The Storage Auction Guide

Chuck Jones

Copyright © 2018 Chuck Jones

All rights reserved.

DEDICATION

To God and all His Glory

CONTENTS

Chapter 1	LOCATING THE AUCTIONS	Page 1
Chapter 2	TOOLS OF THE TRADE	Page 3
Chapter 3	BIDDER REGISTRATION	Page 5
Chapter 4	POLICES AND LAWS	Page 7
Chapter 5	WHAT TO EXPECT	Page 9
Chapter 6	WHAT IS BEHIND DOOR #3	Page 13
Chapter 7	DOWNSIDES	Page 17
Chapter 8	PAYMENT	Page 19
Chapter 9	WHAT IS IT WORTH?	Page 21
Chapter 10	WHERE TO SELL	Page 23
Chapter 11	TO TELL THE TRUTH	Page 27
Chapter 12	COST ACCOCIATION	Page 29

ACKNOWLEDGMENTS

I thank my wife for putting up with me bringing tons of other people's stuff into our home to clean, price and box up to sell.

Chapter 1 - Locating the Auctions

When a storage facility has a renter not paying the rent, the manager puts a red lock on the door so the owner cannot enter until the rent is paid. Usually after sixty to ninety days of making all attempts to collect the rent unsuccessfully, the manager has no choice but to put the unit up for auction. Depending on your state laws, the manager has to advertise the date, time and location of the auction.

When searching your local newspaper, you will find many auctions. Among those auctions you will usually also find storage auctions. There are better sources for you to use in finding storage auctions. The best places are websites that specialize in compiling a list of storage auctions, and they can also be sorted by zip code and a radius of X amount of miles around any particular zip code.

There are a lot of websites like auctionzip.com, that will give you access to all the information you need to start your own business of buying storage units. There are other sites, but with all my trials and errors I learned that when you find something that works, you stick with it because for a business to have success, you have to have the right tools.

It is a good idea to call the storage facility before you leave. The renters who's units are up for auction today have until a minute before the auction starts to come in and pay for their unit, and it will not be auctioned off. There have been times where by the time I got to the storage facility, all the renters came in the morning of the auction and paid for their units and so the auction was called off. Most of the time there will still be at least one unit, but usually five to ten units on average that are still up for auction.

Chapter 2 - Tools of the Trade

Now that you have located your first auction you need to get ready for the auction. There are several items that you will need to take with you to every auction. It is very important to always carry a 750 Lumen LED flashlight or better. A better flashlight enables you to see things that others cannot. It gives you an edge on the upcoming bidding process.

A carpenter with a dull chisel becomes useless. Having the right tools for your business is very important. Don't be like the carpenter and instead get the best flashlight you can afford. You can thank me later.

Thinking ahead, when you purchase a storage unit, you are going to need a lock to secure your investment. After you get really good at this, you will carry many locks depending on how many units are being auctioned that day.

Other tools of the trade are large heavy duty trash bags because there will be trash. My enclosed trailer always has a place for ten empty plastic tubs because the boxes in the unit sometimes fall apart and many times there are small items just thrown in the unit.

I always carry a magnifying glass so when I find jewelry I like to know if it is real or not.

Before you can get your deposit back, you must sweep the unit clean so keep that broom and dust pan handy.

Other items you may or may not need, include a hundred watt light bulb to replace the burnt out bulb in the unit, especially if you are going to be there after dark. If you have a trailer, it would be a good idea to have a dolly/hand truck for the heavier items.

There are times that I use moving blankets to protect the nicer items from getting scratches or dents. I usually keep ten of them in the trailer.

Until you get to know the managers at these storage facilities, you should call to ask them what type of payments do they take and to find out if the auction is still scheduled for the next morning. Most of the storage facilities I go to only accept cash, so make sure you have plenty of cash.

Chapter 3 - Bidder Registration

When arriving to the storage facility, the security gate will be open on auction day. You can just drive in and find somewhere to park. I like to park along the back fence because if you park in front of a unit and that unit is up for auction ... Well, let's just say it's best to stay out of the way.

Not all, but most facilities require you to register. There is no fee to register for an auction, but you may be asked to provide your name, address, phone number and your tax exempt status. Or just your name only, unless you win a unit, upon which they will get all the personal information they need.

You don't have to worry about the previous owner contacting you trying to get their stuff back, because the storage facility is not allowed to give out your personal information without your consent.

To recap, before you get out of your vehicle, make sure you have your driver's license, your top of the line flashlight, along with your lock and key or multiple locks if you're feeling lucky.

Some auctioneers will either have you sign or initial a policy agreement or they will verbally announce the policies just before the bidding begins on the first unit. I will give more details about the normal policies in the next chapter.

Depending on the size of the unit, there will be a cleanout deposit. Smaller units are usually around $50.00 and larger units have up to a $100.00 deposit, which you will get back after you have cleaned the unit.

I travel at least a seventy five mile radius and I like to set my GPS the night before so it is ready as soon as I am ready to go.

CHAPTER 4 - Polices and Laws

Not all auctioneers and storage facilities have the same policies. Some of the policies and laws may include:

1. You must be at least eighteen to bid.

2. You must register in order to bid, buyers must have current, valid, photo I.D.

3. Applicable sales tax will apply unless buyer supplies a copy of the sales tax exempt form prior to payment.

4. No Smoking, No consumption of Alcohol and children must be supervised at all times.

5. All sales are absolutely finale and sold (as is where is) with no exceptions.

6. A cleaning deposit of ($ X amount) is due at the time of payment.

Cleaning deposits are refundable if units are cleaned out and broom swept within the allotted time. (Generally 24 to 72 hours) If not, the buyer forfeits deposit and will not be allowed to bid on future units. Most managers will work with you if you need more time, as long as you let them know in advance.

Buyers may not use the storage facility dumpsters. This means that everything in the unit including the dust, must be hauled off the storage facilities property.

In the event of disputed bids on bid closing, the auctioneer's decision is final. Don't argue. Just in case I did not make it clear, **DON'T ARGUE**.

The Storage facility and or the auctioneer reserve the right to cancel any auction without prior notice. This means that when you get to the auction, there may be no auction, even if you call the day before and were told the auction is tomorrow. Out of the many years that I have been going to storage auctions, only one auction was completely canceled by the time I arrived.

Chapter 5 - What to Expect

You can expect anywhere from five to fifty people showing up at any given storage auction.

Here's the scoop on the bidders. Out of 50 bidders, there will be at least five that don't bid, they just like watching. Then there are about ten to fifteen that only bid on the small units because all they have for transportation is a regular car.

I would say about ten are specific bidders, meaning they are looking for something in particular and they want nothing to do with a regular looking unit.

Out of the twenty left, it now breaks down on a financial level. Meaning fifteen of them will never bid more than five hundred dollars, which leaves about five bidders who are considered competition.

Two factors come into play with the big boys. Even though these bidders play on a much higher financial field, the lack of money can still play a roll, depending how many units they bought in the last three or four days. For example, if they have twenty thousand tied up in storage units they may be a little reluctant to drop another two thousand on one or two more units.

Another dynamic that seems to make its way into the scheme of factoring, is the ability to handle the amount of product. Even when you have a warehouse, a lot of items will need to be cleaned or repaired and must be stored until the time is right. The warehouse can get full and therefore this limits the ability to purchase more. You may be only looking for units that can go straight to an auction house where it will go up for auction thereby limiting the need for a warehouse.

There are many auctions that are called caravan auctions, which means that there are two to five storage facilities all having auctions on the same day by the same auctioneer, and it is usually the same company. For example Jack Rabbit or any large storage company that has multiple facilities in the area.

So it will start off at facility (A) and after the auction is over, it will take a little time for the auctioneer and the storage manager to collect the money and complete everyone's paperwork, usually fifteen to thirty minutes. Then everyone drives over to the next auction at facility (B) and the same process happens at each of the other facilities (C), (D) and (E).

Something you will notice, is that the amount of bidders change over the course of the day. If bidder (1) buys two units at the first auction and two more at the second auction, there will be a good chance that bidder (1) will not show up at the rest of the auctions. Occasionally, a new bidder will show up in the middle or end of the caravan, but overall it seems that most of the time, there are less bidders at the last auction, which is better for anyone bidding on units during the last auction. If you are just starting out in the storage auction bidding process, I would suggest on your first two units, you stick with the smaller units like the 5x5 or smaller.

The smaller units will give you a chance to have a better understanding of how the whole process works. I have a few success stories on the smaller units. You just might be surprised what people can stuff in those small units. Someone could easily put a Harley Davidson in there with a lot of old clothes piled up so high that nobody could ever guess that there is a Harley under all those clothes.

One other thing I should mention. In just about every unit, there will be a lot of items that you can use for yourself. Items like household products that you normally buy are now abundantly available. It has been many years since I have had to purchase Windex, bleach, steel wool pads, brooms, vacuum cleaners, CDs, DVDs, Computers, laptops, and many other products.

Chapter 6 - What's Behind Door #3

When the door is opened, sometimes you will see a packed unit and sometimes there may only be one item. This is where the rubber hits the road. It does help to know what you are looking at because it will help determine how much you will bid on what you see.

More times than not, when people pack up boxes, they will write on the box the contents in the box. Some of the descriptions you will see are: Johnny's toys, kitchen, lamps, fragile, books and so on. (you get the drift.)

Most of the time if the box says china or toys, that is what you will find, but I have to warn you, it is not always the case. Sometimes, people re-use old boxes, so the box that says "china" on it, (and it probably did have china in it before they decided to re-use it) actually has some old dirty socks in it instead.

That illustration can also be reversed. The box can read "Johnny's socks" (and at one point, probably the last move, it did have Johnny's socks in it,) but now there is grandma's sterling silverware in Johnny's old socks box, and they just did not re-label the box.

This can also happen with new factory labeled boxed and boxes with pictures on them, like a seventy two inch flat screen TV. (A lot of dirty clothes can fit in one of those big TV boxes.) I actually have used those big TV boxes for large pictures or large mirrors the last time I moved.

Most of the time when you see those big black trash bags, they are usually full of clothes, unless they are designer top of the line name brand, you will be best to just donate them.

Here is the kicker. My two best purchases ever, were two ten by thirty units full of nothing but boxes. Both units were owned by the same person, who was a big time collector of many things. I found out that the previous owner had some serious health problems and died. There was no junk in either of these units, the boxes were stacked from front to back, side to side and from the floor to the ceiling.

I can thank God for placing the girl at the auction who blurted out for all to hear, "Those could be all empty boxes." Which I know her comment had to have put that thought into the minds of all the bidders because it really could have been all empty boxes!

Out of all the years of buying storage units, this was a massive find. I just don't believe it will ever happen again, but on the other hand, I learned to "never say never" because you never know. I have to say, these two units spoiled me and now when I see a nice unit, I just don't see it the same way as I used to.

OK, getting back to the normal units. What you will usually see in most units are black bags and boxes. And identifiable items like furniture, appliances both large and small, and yard tools such as lawn mowers, weed eaters and blowers. These are easier to form an idea of worth because you can see a lot of the main inventory.

Once you get more experienced, you will look for items that will tell you if the unit belonged to a white collar or a blue collar worker, young or old, male, female or a family. Having knowledge of what type of person owned the unit will help you decide whether you want the unit or not and also will help in determining how much you are willing to bid.

Please never forget that you should only bid on items that you can actually see. I really need to pound it in your head. If you see a sixty inch flat screen TV box, the chance of an actual sixty inch TV being in the box is slim because they are heavy duty boxes that are great for storing and transporting large pictures. Or in the case of one that I found which was packed with coat hangers.

Don't assume that major appliances are in good working order. Just because you would not pay a monthly storage bill to store a bunch of non-working appliances, doesn't mean that someone else wouldn't. Remember, you cannot judge a book by its cover nor can you know what is in a box by the picture on it or what is written on it.

Most units are messy and a few are nice and neat. Just because a unit is well kept, does not mean that there is anything of value, although it does usually mean that the items are in good condition. The messy units can easily be more valuable than a clean unit.

There is a TV show about storage units that I have never watched because I did see snippets in commercials, and just by seeing those snippets, I formed an opinion of a "false reality," that looked like a bunch of fake hype. Reminded me of all the "fake news."

I would say you might have a really good find in one out of fifty units, and for the most part, you will make a decent living from the business of buying storage units. Even looking at this as a business venture, it would be neglectful not to mention the fun factor. It is like a treasure hunt, because you don't know what you will find.

Chapter 7 - The Downsides

There are possible health hazards to some people, mainly mold, but there are other things you should keep in mind. Do not reach into boxes and try to feel around the bottom to see if there is anything good buried under everything else. You never know what you could be putting your hand into.

One time I was reaching in a large box feeling around and kept feeling something weird, and when I pulled my hand out it was covered in blood. I was moving my hand all around a bunch of razor blades. It actually did not hurt while it was slicing the "beegeebees" out of my hand, it just felt strange because I never felt that before. Just don't do it, learn from my stupidity. I'm glad to share it with you because if I can prevent something like this from happening to just one person, it will make the humiliation of talking about my stupidity worth it.

I have found small dead animals and dead rats. I even found a dead person one time! Luckily, he had been cremated and it just looked like a box of crunched up cement. Did I mention cockroaches? OMG. The last thing you want to do is bring cockroaches home. Sometimes it might be better to set off a fogger right after you purchase the unit and go back the next day to load everything.

Although I have never needed it, I always carry a small pistol for protection. So far I have had no problems, but I don't want to be in a unit I just bought and the previous owner of the unit shows up and is not happy to see me rummaging through what he feels is still his unit. I'm just saying, it's better to be safe than sorry.

Chapter 8 - Payment

When you win a unit, you must pay before you can start going through the unit. After the last unit is auctioned, all the winners will meet at the rental office. Most facilities will only allow one winning bidder in the office at a time while the others wait outside. Don't just assume you can whip out your credit card to pay for your unit. Most facilities only accept cash while others will process debit and credit cards. They do not process checks, so be sure you know what types of payment they use before bidding.

If you want to claim "tax exempt," you should bring your re-sale certificate with you and they will have it filed, so you do not have to bring your re-sale certificate each time. Your payment will consist of the bid amount, tax, (unless you claim tax exempt) and a security deposit. Some auctioneers may charge a small buyers commission, usually ten percent. After your payment has been processed, they will give you a receipt and a temporary code for the entrance gate that is good for the amount of hours they allotted you to clean out the unit.

If you purchase a large thirty or forty foot unit, they will work with you a little on the time frame for getting the unit cleaned out. Most contracts will offer forty eight to seventy two hours to clean them out. If it is taking longer than expected, and they are done working with you, you will have to pay for a month's rent. Most facilities will cut you a deal by offering you half off the regular rental cost.

Chapter 9 - What is it worth?

My favorite tool to use is eBay's advance search. It will show all the recently sold items. So if you want to sell a "THING - A-MA - JIG" or a "WHATCHA-MACALL-IT," just go to eBay, and look over at the top right corner, and right next to the search button, you will see the word "Advance."

Click on the word "Advance" and on the next page, you will see the top box that says, "Enter Keywords or Item Number." Type a description of the item that you want to find out what it is worth, and then just below the search button, click the little square box next that says "Sold Listings." Then go back up to the search button and click "search." It will bring up all the recently sold items of whatever you typed in. Any product you are selling is worth what someone is willing and able to pay for it.

This advance search will give you a good idea of what people are willing to pay for your item. It is best to look at the auction style listings because they will be more accurate. The "Buy Now" auctions are not as accurate because sellers could be under selling the item's true value. When you see bidders bidding against each other, where it stops is the most accurate worth value.

There are other web sites like Worth Point which you can use also to identify an item that you are unfamiliar with. (There have been plenty of items in my hand with me looking at it, thinking,

"What is this thing?") It's actually fun when you discover what something is, what it is worth, and other information such as its history and so forth.

Some Online Price Guides are:

www.beckett.com/price-guides (for baseball cards and others.)

https://comicspriceguide.com/ (for comic books.)

VinylBeat.com & Popsike.com (for vinyl records.)

www.discogs.com (It is the best place to go to find prices and other information on records.)

www.crawforddirect.com/worth.html (this is a great place to go to find the value of most items.)

http://www.zeppy.io/index.php?country_code=us

(You can find just about anything your looking for at zeppy's)

Chapter 10 - Where to Sell

Now that you have won your first auction, your next concern is to make a profit. The type of item will determine what avenue you try first. Let's look at places to sell and look at the costs of selling.

You can take items to an auction company and let them sell for you, but you will pay a fee. Most auction companies around my area charge thirty to thirty five percent. If you find a company that generally can pull in top dollar for the items they auction, this route may be right for you.

When you start to deal with a high volume of storage units, the less profit per unit is more affordable than just buying one unit at a time. I am more into "turn-around" than trying to hold out for top dollar. However, if there are a few high dollar items then I will put in more effort to realizing it's full potential.

Online auctions like eBay are good for the small items, but it can be a lot of work. You will need to take pictures, create an ad describing the item, research the asking price, packaging the item and taking it to the post office. The cost of selling on eBay usually involves 10% to eBay, 2% to Papal and small listing fees depending on if you list more than 50 items. The cost of selling on eBay is still considerably lower than running your items through an auction company, plus you have control over the selling price.

Consignment shops are a way to control the selling price vs. an auction company. You price your item and it gets placed in a retail outlet like an antique or thrift store, and when it sells, you pay around 30% to 35%. This is what I do with most of my antiques and unusual items.

Flea markets are another way to sell, but keep in mind the money you save on selling costs usually is lost because of price reduction. People that go to flea markets are looking for and expecting a good deal for them, therefore your prices will need to be lowered for this venue of selling.

The best items for flea markets are personal products like hair care, cosmetics, shampoo, clothing, cheap nick knacks and other small items. You also could just sell in bulk to flea market sellers. I use an indoor flea market. This is where I take all the items that I used to give away or throw away.

Craig's list is a free way to sell. It easier than eBay because there is no packaging and shipping. The only downside to this method is you are inviting people that you don't know to come onto your property. Thieves and other wrong doers also use this venue for their business of (STEALING).

They can pretend to be interested in what you are selling, while at the same time it gives them the opportunity to scope out your property so that they can figure out if it worth coming back at night to steal from you. When I am selling something on Craig's list and a potential buyer is coming over to look at it, I take it out by the street to limit their ability to scope out my operation, plus if they actually buy it, it is right there ready to load.

I throw all of the undesirable pots, pans, broken lawn chairs, or any other metal that is not in sellable condition in a pile behind one of my storage workshops. Regarding the old tube TVs, I take the backs off of and remove the copper wiring and thick copper wire around the tube. After the pile grows to the size of a trailer load, I load the trailer and take it to the local scrap yard. With copper running around $2.50 a pound and aluminum at .50 cents a pound, it is a way to make a few bucks on the things you cannot sell anywhere else.

There are many other ways to sell your items, but these are my top five best sources for moving products and getting top dollar.

Other ways may be selling to friends, advertising in your local newspaper, building your own online website, etsy.com, amazon.com, Facebook, yard sales, local community billboards, etc. and any other way that you have observed that other people using.

Remember that a clean item is more appealing to a potential buyer. Cleaners and other products you may want to keep on hand are: bleach, lime away or CLR, stainless steel cleaner, Goo gone, paint remover, and other typical cleaners.

It is also a good idea to have steel wool pads, wire brush, touch up paint pens, furniture touch up pens, shoe polish, Murphy's Oil Soap, Old English for scratches in furniture and many other useful ways to clean, using products like white vinegar, baking soda, rubbing alcohol and salt are some of the ones I use most often.

Chapter 11 - To Tell the Truth

Honesty is the best policy, but you have to remember, not everyone is as honest as you. I'm NOT going to call anyone a liar, but I will tell you the story and let you come up with your own conclusions.

I bought a unit and when I was going through the contents, I came across an unopened loaf of bread. It felt fresh, so I looked at the expiration date and it had not expired yet. Because I know the rules and laws on unpaid storage units, this fresh loaf of bread was bothering me so much, I put it in a black trash bag and went to the office. I asked the manager "What is the time frame between the time you put a red lock on a unit because a renter is behind on payment, and the time the unit is auctioned? The manager said "It is seventy to ninety days," so I said, "So this unit has been locked up with your red lock for at least the past seventy days?" The manager replied "Yes," to which I replied "So let me get this straight, nobody has been in this unit since you put the red lock on it seventy days ago?" The manager said "That's right." So I pulled out the loaf of bread and placed it on the counter and asked them to look at the expiration date, then I asked them "Is it possible that just before you put the red lock on, the renter bought a loaf of bread into the unit that had an expiration date that was good for more than seventy days?" Of course they could not explain it, so what do you think?

I have no firsthand knowledge, but I have heard that some storage facilities actually pack units and then auction them off!

How this works is when people move out, they may leave one or two items (and this happens all the time) so management takes all the unwanted items and puts them in a particular unit until it is full and then has it auctioned off. These units may also have trash from the dumpsters.

The only reason I am telling this unconfirmed story is that it would explain how someone could find a loaf of bread that has not expired for seventy days!

Chapter 12 - Cost Association

So what does all this really cost? Actual cost depends on whether you are in the storage business solely, or part time along with a regular job. By having a regular job, a large portion of non-direct cost can be divided between your job and your storage buying business.

For an example, the cost associated with owning a truck and trailer can be proportionally between your job and your business. The trailer is most likely 100% business so let's look at the cost of your truck.

If the annual cost of your transportation is $8,500.00, you can divide that cost by figuring the mileage you rack up traveling to and from your job, subtracting personal use, like going to the grocery store, etc. and by dividing these figures into the total annual millage. This will give you a good estimate of your business cost of transportation.

Out of ten storage auctions, there may be three or four in which I spent time and gas money for nothing because the units did not appeal to me or the bidding went too high for my calculation and I ended up leaving empty handed.

One way to help offset the cost of looking at storage auctions is by going online to sites like https://www.storageunitauctionlist.com http://www.storageauctions.com https://storagestuff.bid

These websites work like storagetreasures.com. You sign up and receive access to a list of upcoming auctions in your area.

The time it takes to look at online storage auctions as opposed to going to them in person, is cut by more than fifty percent, plus it saves on gas, and wear and tear on your truck. When bidding online, the only time you use your truck and trailer is when you actually win a bid and need to pick it up.

Now if you decided to do nothing but online bidding, there are some things to take into consideration. If you are only doing storage auctions part time, the online bidding may be perfect for you.

If you do this line of work full time, you will find that onsite auctions are going on somewhere all the time, but online auctions have periods where there are no auctions taking place at all.

The way I do it is, if there is an online auction, and an onsite auction the same day, I prefer to do the online action and I go to the onsite auctions only when there are no online auctions.

There is one downside to online auctions which is even if you win the auction, if the current owner shows up to pay for the unit before you can get there, you may show up just to be told, "Sorry but the unit was paid for by the unit owner." Although this has never happened to me, I'm just letting you know that it is possible.

About the Author

I make buying storage units as declared within the Declaration of Independence nothing more than my ordinary business. We hold these truths to be self-evident, that all men are created equal, that they are endowed by their Creator with certain unalienable Rights, that among these are Life, Liberty and the pursuit of Happiness. My pursuit of happiness is owning private property, private businesses, private transportation and to declare my self-governance. This book is a testament of my private business and that no entity/person has my permission to copy, change or re-write this book in any form. This book is for informational purposes only and the content within shall only be used in accordance with the laws that govern all persons.

All Rights Reserved

www.ingramcontent.com/pod-product-compliance
Lightning Source LLC
Chambersburg PA
CBHW030102230526
45471CB00003B/1214